WE SMILE WHEN WE EAT!

Eric A. Kelly

Published by

Eric A. Kelly

MIAMI, FLORIDA

This work is intended to educate, inspire and build moral character. All drawings are part of the authors imagination.

ISBNs:
978-1-64008-621-0 (paperback)
978-1-64008-622-7 (ebook)

Interior and cover design: Gary A. Rosenberg
www.garyarosenberg.com

Printed in the United States of America

This book is dedicated to making sure that
every child is given a bright and healthy future,
knowing that the development of their lives
will drive the world in the right direction.

Hello boys and girls. Today I want you guys to help me share with the world the story of why we smile when we eat.

We smile because our hearts are
happy, joyful and loving.

We smile because we are young kings and queens.
We smile because we are pretty and handsome.

We smile because our faces light up the
room like the moon; and our teeth are
the stars—even if we don't have any.

We smile because we are loved by family and friends and because we know how to give love back.

5

We smile because the world is our
playground for growth. We open our arms
like the birds and soar to greatness.

We smile because each of us are different colors, like crayons, but we share and fit together just like the box we came out of.

We smile because when we are home, our dads and
moms teach us from the start, so when we get
to school, we help the teachers with our part.

We smile through the learning
process because, through
the process, we are getting
stronger and stronger.

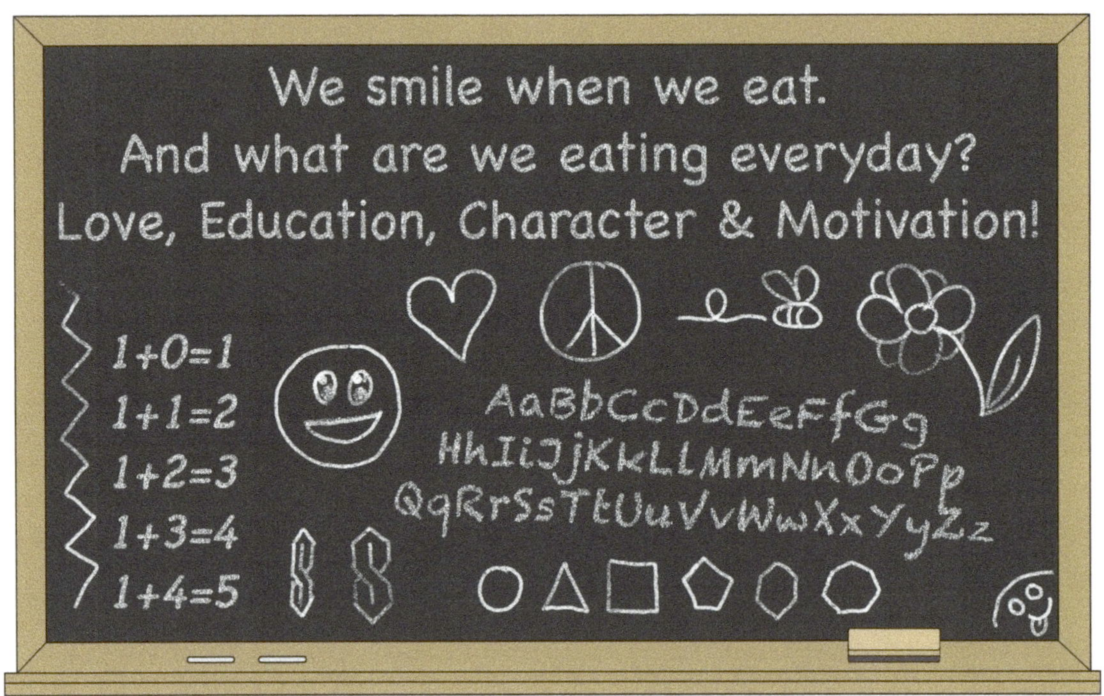

And we smile because our favorite subjects
are math, reading, writing and art!

We smile when it's breakfast time because
it's the healthy part of the morning that
gets the brain and body functioning.

We smile when it's lunch time because we
know the day is halfway through, and a little
juice plus fruit will give us an extra boost.

We smile when it's dinner time because
family time evolves the mind.

We smile when we watch TV, play sports, swim,
and dance. Because through our eyes, we can see
and be thankful that everyone is given a chance.

So last, but not least, the reason we smile
when we eat comes from love, building character,
encouraging, sharing, and dancing. Those are the
steps to a better world, young boys and girls.

Keeping Track of What I Eat

This page is for example only—use a notebook or app to record what you eat and drink each day for a week.

Breakfast: ____

____

Lunch: ____

____

Dinner: ____

____

Snacks: ____

____

Beverages: ____

____

Discussion Points For Adults and Kids

Now that you have a good idea of what you eat and drink, sit down with a trusted adult and have a little talk . . .

* What are some of my favorite food(s)?

* What do I know about nutrition and proper eating?

* Do I think it's important to eat healthy foods? Why?

* Do I eat three healthy meals each day?

* Does my diet include fresh fruits and vegetables?

* What snacks do I eat? Are they good for my body?

* How do I feel about high-sugar drinks and foods?

* Can I get healthy lunches and/or snacks at school?

* How can I make sure I maintain a healthy diet?

About the Author

Born and raised in Miami, Florida, **Eric A. Kelly** is a two-time self-published author with many other projects slated for 2021. He has been writing professionally since 2010.

Eric has a passion for writing and reading, and loves to write whatever comes to his heart and mind; therefore, he writes in different genres. For this children's book he wanted to write something educational, substance-driven, and fun for young children and parents.